LONDON TRANSPORT

Michael H. C. Baker

Published in Great Britain in 2016 by Shire
Publications Ltd (part of Bloomsbury Publishing Plc),
PO Box 883, Oxford, OX1 9PL, UK.

PO Box 3985, New York, NY 10185-3985, USA.

E-mail: shire@shirebooks.co.uk   www.shirebooks.co.uk

© 2016 Michael H. C. Baker.

A CIP catalogue record for this book is available from
the British Library.

Shire Library no. 799.   ISBN-13: 978 0 74781 429 0

Michael H. C. Baker has asserted his right under
the Copyright, Designs and Patents Act, 1988, to be
identified as the author of this book.

Typeset in Garamond Pro and Gill Sans.

Printed in China through Worldprint Ltd.

16 17 18 19 20   10 9 8 7 6 5 4 3 2 1

COVER IMAGE
Front cover design and photography by Peter Ashley. A
detail from Leyland Bus RTL1076. Back cover detail:
Radiator badge from a London Country bus.

TITLE PAGE IMAGE
A DMS-type bus crosses Southwark Bridge heading
south on route 95, c. 1971. Warehouse buildings
line the north bank of the river Thames. In the
background, the dome of St Paul's Cathedral stands
against the skyline.

CONTENTS PAGE IMAGE
Detail of poster on p.40.

ACKNOWLEDGEMENTS
Images are acknowledged as follows:

© TfL from the London Transport Museum
Collection, title page and pages 3, 4, 6 (Ashfield, Pick
and Holden), 8, 11, 12 (top), 16, 20, 22, 23 (top), 24,
27, 29, 31, 34, 36 (top), 38 (top), 40, 42, 46 (top),
48, 51 (bottom), 54, 62.

Dutch National Archives, page 6 (Herbert Morrison).

All remaining images are from the author's collection.

Shire Publications is supporting the Woodland Trust, the UK's leading woodland conservation charity, by funding the dedication of trees.

CONTENTS

HOW IT BEGAN

I N 1933 THE London Passenger Transport Board (LPTB), commonly known as London Transport, was created to rationalise transport in the capital; in 1948 it became the London Transport Executive, and in the twenty-first century it has continued its challenging work as Transport for London (TfL). Since the beginning of the twentieth century many had seen the necessity of a unified authority to oversee public transport in the capital, and things began to move in this direction in 1924 with the passing of the London Traffic Act; it was driven forward by Herbert Morrison, Minister of Transport in the Labour government of 1929 and later leader of the London County Council (LCC).

Opposite bottom: Westminster Bridge, c. 1935, with five trams of LCC origin, dating from between 1910 and 1930. The first and third metal-bodied cars are heading for the Kingsway Subway.

Right: Harry Beck's iconic diagrammatic Underground map of 1933, an inspiration for a host of spin-offs worldwide.

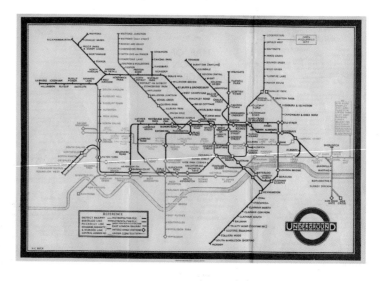

The biggest player by far prior to 1933 was the Combine, which owned most of the Underground and Tube railways, a number of tram companies, and the London General Omnibus Company (LGOC). Trams had a significant presence on the streets of London, particularly those owned by

the London County Council, which regarded the tram as the transport of the working man and his family, serving as it did the densely populated areas north and south of the Thames, where the busiest docks in the world and large numbers of factories were located.

One of the mammoth Leyland Titanic six-wheelers, dating from 1929, of the City Bus Company at Victoria. A rival to the AEC Renown, it was soon withdrawn by the LPTB.

Other services were provided by three companies operating in west and north London and eight municipalities. There were also many small bus and motor coach operators, although a number of these, seeing the creation of the LPTB as imminent, had sold out to the Combine.

Chairman and head of the LPTB was the charismatic figure of Albert Stanley, 1st Baron Ashfield. Working alongside him was Frank Pick, chief executive from 1933 until 1940. They had long worked together. Lord Ashfield, headhunted from Detroit, had been appointed general manager of the Combine at the age of thirty-three in 1907; he had then become managing director in 1910, and was knighted four years later.

Pick had come to London from the North Eastern Railway and was also to have

The four men most instrumental in the creation of the London Passenger Transport Board (clockwise from top left): Lord Ashfield, chairman; Frank Pick, managing director; James Holden, architect; and Herbert Morrison, Minister of Transport in the 1929 Labour government.

experience of public transport across the Atlantic, having been sent by Lord Ashfield to New York shortly after the end of the First World War. He had been surprised by the number of commuters there:

The rush hour in New York is almost unbelievable. I thought I had seen overcrowding on the east end of the District Railway. I fancied I had seen too many people in a car after a Chelsea football match … but it was not until I was in New York that I realized that the London public … has not yet learned the first word in overcrowding.

Speaking in 1936, Pick defined his role, and that of Lord Ashfield, in the LPTB: '… the Chairman … is the inspiration of all that we have done…who gets on comfortably by intuition – that is his job. The other who gets on by industry – that is my job.'

On the creation of the LPTB, Pick was appointed managing director. Many years later Anthony Bull CBE, a vice-chairman of the later London

Morden in the late 1920s, just before the Tube arrived.

Transport Board, was interviewed about Lord Ashfield and Pick, having worked closely with both; he spoke of 'two very different personalities' but said that 'both recognised each was necessary to the other. Lord Ashfield … was a skilled political operator … you had this sense of an electric personality. Pick trained as a solicitor but … developed into an outstanding administrator … a perfectionist in an imperfect world.' Talking to the chief officers of the LPTB, Pick told them, 'Do not be afraid of a spice of vice, a spark of irrationality, a fondness for inconsistency, a flash of genius.'

Pick had an extraordinary flair for design and, after his death in 1940, Nikolaus Pevsner described him as 'the greatest patron of the arts whom this century has so far produced in England.' A devout Congregationalist, Pick had no interest in honours, refusing both a knighthood and a peerage.

These two men were faced with the mammoth task of bringing together all the disparate elements which made up LPTB into one, and it is to their eternal credit that by 1939 they had achieved this, backed up by many gifted subordinates and a work force that, by and large, was proud to serve the transport needs of the capital and its surrounding areas.

No wonder the London Passenger Transport Board was in a hurry to get rid of its trams. This primitive, open-top, open-fronted, four-wheeler had entered service with Croydon Corporation in 1911. Seen at Crystal Palace in 1934, it was replaced when trolleybuses took over the following year.

1879

LONDON TRANSPORT IS SEEKING POWERS FROM PARLIAMENT TO CONVERT 90 MILES OF ITS TRAMWAYS TO TROLLEYBUS ROUTES

1933

ORGANISING TRANSPORT IN LONDON

WHEN THE LPTB began operations on 1 July 1933, it covered an area of 1,550 square miles which had a population of over nine million. Although car ownership was increasing rapidly, the vast majority of those 9.4 million depended on public transport to get to and from work, school, the shops and wherever else fancy or necessity took them. Towns in the far north and west of this area, such as Bishop Stortford, Luton, Dunstable, High Wycombe and Slough, were well into the Home Counties, and, to the south and east, those such as Gravesend, Tonbridge, East Grinstead and Horsham were halfway to the sea. Beyond this there were another 436 square miles in which the LPTB could operate

Opposite:
A poster promoting what would eventually become the largest trolleybus fleet in the world, featuring the London United prototype No.61 of 1933.

Pedestrians scurry between E1 and E3 trams and ex-LGOC and Thomas Tilling STs in the heart of Brixton, c. 1937, many of them customers of Woolworth's 'nothing more than 6d' store, a feature of just about every English high street in those days.

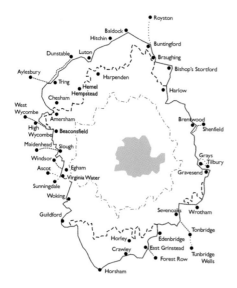

The area served by the London Passenger Transport Board from 1933 onwards.

if the traffic commissioners saw fit to grant it licences. This resulted in a quirky system in which, for example, Green Line coaches (and not County Area buses) served Tunbridge Wells, which was otherwise exclusively Maidstone and District territory; meanwhile, County Area buses (not Green Line coaches) reached Forest Row on the edge of the Ashdown Forest, otherwise covered by Maidstone and District, and Luton was the only town served both by the LPTB and corporation buses.

The road transport section of the LPTB was divided into three sections: the Central Area; the Country Area; and Trams and Trolleybuses. The Central Area consisted of central London, the inner and much of the outer suburbs – exactly the same area served by London General buses – while the Country Area overlapped with

The former MET centre-entrance Feltham No.331, LT No.2168, of 1930, and the only surviving example of this groundbreaking design still in passenger service, seen at the National Tram Museum, Crich.

the outer suburbs and the rural or semi-rural areas beyond. Central Area vehicles were painted red and what was described as 'broken white' with silver roofs and black lining, which was pretty much a continuation of the General livery. Indeed, for a few months newly overhauled buses actually bore the General fleet name.

Country Area vehicles had a two-tone dark and light green colour scheme with black lining and silver roofs. Far and away the largest contributors to the Country Area were East Surrey and National. The General had worked closely with both: it had acquired the former in 1929, and, since 1921, had supplied buses and was in charge of the garages and equipment of the latter. The works were at Reigate, although overhauls were soon transferred to Chiswick.

Trams and Trolleybuses was the third road-operating department and enjoyed a considerable degree of autonomy, being run largely by ex-employees of London County Council Tramways. The works were situated at Charlton. Most trams consisted of variations on the outdated London County Council E1 theme which originated in Edwardian times, even though production hadn't ended until 1930. C. J. Spencer of the Metropolitan Electric Tramways, part of the Combine, was responsible for London's only fleet of truly modern tramcars, the one hundred magnificent, mould-breaking Felthams.

Spencer took up a senior position with the LPTB but soon left, Ashfield and Pick having made it clear that there was no future for the tram in London. With the impending end

LONDON'S TRAMWAYS

STREATHAM
COMMON AND THE ROOKERY
TRAM SERVICES
EMBANKMENT·16·18·22·24
VICTORIA·20 CITY·6·10

A Pick-inspired poster. Only tram routes 16 and 18 actually passed Streatham Common, which was a ten-minute walk from St Leonard's Church, where the other routes diverged towards Tooting.

LORD MAYOR'S
SHOW

A Henry
Perry poster
advertising
the 1935 Lord
Mayor's Show.
It has been
something of
a tradition,
carried on to
the present day,
that London
Transport (now
Transport
for London)
participates in
this November
event.

of the tram there was little incentive to improve or modify the system and the cars. A few of the most decrepit municipal ones were replaced by surplus LCC ones, and even those for imminent withdrawal were repainted in LPTB livery. Anomalies such as more than one route carrying the same number remained until trolleybuses took over or were simply abandoned.

The fleet consisted of 5,405 buses, 2,565 tramcars, sixty-one trolleybuses, 464 coaches and 2,448 Underground trains. There was a fair degree of standardisation within the bus fleet, the vast majority of vehicles being of AEC manufacture, although there were several hundred Leylands and a sprinkling of just about every other make ever conjured up within the UK. In 1933, if a bus or coach lasted ten years, it had done well and the LPTB drew up plans to remove all non-standard vehicles as soon as possible; by 1939 this had largely been achieved.

Trains could be divided into three categories. These were the deep level Tubes, much narrower than the norm; those working on the District line which were built to the same dimensions as main-line vehicles; and those working on the Metropolitan

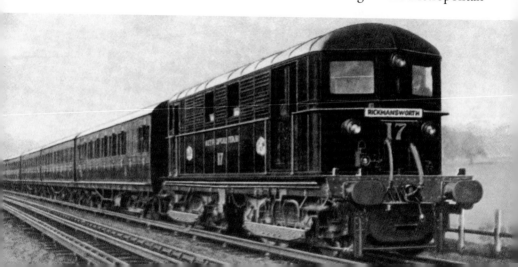

line. Many of the latter were scarcely distinguishable from their District line counterparts but they belonged to a company which considered itself, at least in some respects, more of a main-line operator than an underground one, serving as it did some choice areas of Metroland, still semi-rural although getting less so with each passing year, with rural Buckinghamshire beyond. Amersham, Chesham and Aylesbury were served by brown compartment stock carriages, scarcely distinguishable from those operated by the London and North Eastern Railway out of Marylebone, whose tracks they shared, and were hauled by electric locomotives south of Ricksmansworth, and by steam engines beyond. There were even two Pullman cars, which took business men into the City in the morning, brought them back in the evening and in between conveyed their wives to the West End for tea and shopping.

One of the principal tasks of the newly formed LPTB was to coordinate all its services, and this mammoth undertaking was tackled with enthusiasm. There was much to do in the Country Area, particularly in reaching agreement with the neighbouring companies of Maidstone and District, Southdown, Aldershot and District, Thames Valley and Eastern National where some routes were lost or adjusted and others gained. One of the most important changes was to renumber all routes into a logical system. Thus, routes north of the Thames were put into the 3xx series; those to the

Greenwich Power Station. Built by the LCC in 1906, it provided power for London's trams and, later, trolleybuses, until this responsibility was taken over by the National Grid.

Opposite bottom: Metropolitan line trains serving the desirable Buckinghamshire towns of Amersham and Chesham were composed of compartment stock carriages hauled as far as Rickmansworth by electric locomotives (and thence by steam), as shown in this postcard from the 1930s.

The last of the archaic-looking NS-type double-deck buses was withdrawn in 1937, despite improvements of pneumatic tyres and covered tops. The officially preserved example is seen here in 1971 at the old Museum of British Transport at Clapham.

south, 4xx. This fitted into the overall LPTB scheme: Central Area double-deck routes ranged from 1 to 199; single-deck ones were in the 2xx series; and, as the trolleybus system gradually expanded, the 5xx and 6xx series were used. Tram routes always remained in a separate category which could result in bus and tram routes using the same numbers running alongside each other but presumably it was assumed that all passengers would be able to tell the difference between a bus and a tram. Green Line services were, illogically, given letters; but as there were considerably more routes than numbers of the alphabet, this meant that some also had to have a number suffix. It was only post-1945 that the sensible solution of putting them into the 700 series was employed.

One of the most important departments was the Traffic Office, which kept a close eye on every route, monitoring passenger loadings at various times of the day and constantly making adjustments to schedules accordingly. Any proposed changes would be put out to public consultation. Although car ownership increased throughout the 1933–9 period, so did bus travel in the LPTB area – from 1.9 billion passengers in 1933–4 to 2.2 billion in 1938–9.

In his book *Frank Pick's London* Oliver Green observes that 'London Transport's path of modernisation and improvement in its first five years of existence was remarkable.' In a talk to senior management in 1936 Pick noted:

> The London Passenger Transport Board has become an accepted institution in London in three years. It has become established in the remembrance and regard of Londoners, I almost think in their affections. We are part of London. That is a great achievement.

TF77 of 1939, a joint Leyland/ LPTB design of Green Line coach with underfloor engine but retaining a half-cab layout.

THE WORLD'S FINEST URBAN TRANSPORT SYSTEM

OVER THE YEARS since the first standard London General double-decker, the B type of 1910, which had seats for thirty-four passengers, engineers had striven to increase capacity within the strict dimensions laid down by the Metropolitan Police. The LPTB's standard double-deck bus throughout the 1930s was the AEC Regent; the earliest example, the ST type, dating from 1929, seated forty-eight passengers. However, the police allowed a six-wheel chassis to be longer, and contemporary with the ST was the LT Renown, which could seat sixty passengers. Then, in 1932, regulations were eased which meant that the Regent STL type of 1932 could also seat sixty, although in rather cramped conditions. Later STLs seated fifty-six, and this number was the norm right through the 1930s and '40s and into the 1950s.

Opposite:
A late 1930s Underground poster promoting the notion of travel being an education.

A crew member of ST839 takes a breather at the Thornton Heath Pond terminus of route 59. A Thomas Tilling AEC Regent, it was rebuilt and modernised by the LPTB but retained its open staircase.

STL 2377 in 1939 with the route number indicator on the roof.

The only surviving Thomas Tilling Regent, ST922, at the London Bus Preservation Trust's museum at Brooklands, Surrey.

Certain types were allocated to specific garages and routes but this was a constantly changing scene and it was never the policy, perhaps surprisingly, to allocate the newest buses to the busiest central London routes. The LPTB's attitude was that the regular overhaul of the fleet – virtually annually – and the thoroughness with which this was carried out at Chiswick Works ensured that each bus emerged practically brand new.

The LPTB always liked to display the maximum amount of route, destination and number information that space would allow, both back and front and at the side on its double-deck buses, unlike its trams and trolleybuses, and the later STL, with its number displayed on the roof, epitomised this approach. By the outbreak of the Second World War the highest numbered STL was 2647, the final standard example taking up work on 4 September 1939, the day after war had broken out.

Since the earliest days of the horse bus it was realised that the bus could function as a wonderful moving advertising billboard, and by allowing adverts to be placed at the back and

front beside the destination displays, along the sides and even inside, a great deal of revenue was generated. It was thus most unusual to see a London bus at work clad solely in its basic red and off-white livery. Indeed, some of the adverts seemed to be almost part of the livery, the most famous being the Picture Post eyes placed either side of the front indicators.

For the first thirty years of its existence the motor bus had been powered by a petrol engine but the diesel – or oil engine as it was then called – was shown to be more economical. By the mid 1930s this had become standard in the London fleet, and a number of older buses were refitted accordingly, although petrol engines did not disappear from the London fleet until the early post-war era.

Meanwhile, the LPTB, and Frank Pick in particular, had decided that the tram was outdated, and from 1935 onwards began removing it from the streets of London. However, a good deal of its infrastructure was far from time-expired and therefore it made sense to replace the tram by the smooth, almost silent, very comfortable six-wheel trolleybus.

Although both AEC and Leyland supplied the chassis and a number of different makers built the bodies, the London

The prototype of the huge RT family, RT1 of 1939 (with a later chassis).

trolleybus was highly standardised. Most seated seventy passengers, almost the same as a tram, and by the time the last conversion took place, in 1940, and the last standard trolleybus, No.1721, arrived the following year, there were 1,671 in the fleet, compared with 1,127 trams. Almost all the north London tram routes had been replaced, the exceptions being those which made use of the Kingsway Subway connecting the Embankment with Bloomsbury. Had it not been for the war, the last London tram would have been gone by 1944, but, as it was, 1952 turned out to be the year of its eventual demise, while the trolleybus was to last for a further ten years.

Although we may think of the typical London bus as a big red double-decker, there was a sizeable number of green-painted double- and single-deckers which ran deep into the countryside from the suburbs. The Green Line network dated from 1930, and to operate it the LPTB introduced a large fleet of handsome, well-appointed AEC Regals (the T type), which, although described as coaches were really rather superior buses. In addition, the company worked closely with AEC and Leyland throughout the 1930s to develop alternatives to the traditional half-cab layout in order to increase the seating capacity by putting the engine either under the floor or at the back. The AEC Q, with its horizontal engine placed at the

The new face of urban transport: a Leyland F1 trolleybus and an AEC Q-type Green Line coach, both with LPTB Chiswick-designed bodywork, at Uxbridge shortly after entering service in 1937.

side, could seat up to thirty-seven passengers, compared with around thirty in a T. The Leyland TF also had an underfloor engine, while the short-wheelbase CR's engine was at the rear. Although experimental, the Q and the TF had normal working lives, the Q in particular giving sterling service as a bus in both the Central and Country Areas throughout the war.

Excellent though the standard STL may have been, it was still fairly primitive. There were, for instance, no heaters for either passengers or driver, the latter sitting in his doorless cab, which lacked instrumentation of any sort. Lowering the windows in warm weather involved getting a firm grip on a pinch-type catch, not easily done. The successor of the STL entered service as RT1 in August 1939. Described by Ken Blacker in *RT: the Story of a London Bus* as 'one of the most characterful and well-loved families of bus ever built', there were 4825 RTs alone, to say nothing of the various derivatives. Production ended in 1954.

By 1939 the LPTB had got rid of nearly all the non-standard buses and coaches it had inherited in 1933 and withdrawal of the huge ST and LT fleet would have begun had not the war intervened.

The LPTB had inherited a very varied collection of Tube and surface-type trains. With typical thoroughness they set about designing replacements which, like the motor bus and trolleybus, would become iconic. Just as 1934 was an important

A Circle line train of Metadyne stock, introduced in 1937. Variously known as the O and P stock, these beautiful vehicles constituted one of the best investments the LPTB ever made. The very similar post-war R stock survived until 1983.

One of the 1938 Tube trains, when new. These were the first to have all the electrical and power equipment stowed away beneath the floor thus allowing maximum passenger space. Ahead of their time, they served Londoners for fifty years, rather too long in the end.

year for the trolleybus – when No.62 emerged and was the prototype for a standard which remained in production until 1952 – and 1939 was the year of the prototype RT, so, too, the year of 1938 will be remembered in the history of Tube and surface Underground trains. The Metadyne stock, designed for the Metropolitan and District lines, was fitted with a new control system, developed by Metropolitan Vickers, and was a superb-looking train, streamlined and elegant with its flared sides. As with the single-deck bus, clearing away all equipment to below the floor and thus increasing passenger capacity was the priority for the Tube train, and for the first time this was achieved with the 1938 stock. There are some examples still working seven days a week, far from their original place of operation, in the Isle of Wight.

Which brings us to buildings and the work of James Holden. James Holden was a self-effacing man, who, like Frank Pick, refused a knighthood and all other honours, and perhaps for this reason it is only of late that he has received recognition as one of the greatest British architects of the twentieth century. He not only designed Senate House of London University, London's first skyscraper, but also the LPTB's headquarters at 55 Broadway; but it is perhaps his series of Underground and Tube stations of the 1930s, all still in use, now listed and most sensitively updated but essentially as he designed them, which have fixed for ever his reputation as a great architect.

Examples of his work can be seen in stations such as Cockfosters on the Piccadilly line, Morden on the Northern line and Acton Town on the District line. Holden was never an employee of the LPTB; the stations and other buildings he designed were attributed to the firm of Adams, Holden and

Pearson, of which he was a partner. Holden and Pick had an innate understanding of what constituted good design, and a pencil sketch from Holden was usually sufficient for Pick to give him the go-ahead. Architect Edward Cullinan described Holden's style as 'early excellent Arts and Crafts to … truly modern.' Holden, like Le Corbusier, the Bauhaus architects and Frank Lloyd Wright, held no brief for decoration for decoration's sake. Of course, no architect can ever work in isolation and Holden was the first to acknowledge this, affirming that architecture was collaborative. Among others who made significant contributions were Stanley Heaps, who was an employee of the Combine and the LPTB, and the practices of James and Bywaters, and Wallis, Gilbert and Partners; but Holden led the way. 'A building should be fit for purpose' was his guiding principle, and the passage of time has confirmed the soundness of this approach.

One of James Holden's handsome designs for the Underground, this was Morden, the terminus of the Northern line, at the end of what was then the longest rail tunnel in the world.

Cockfosters Station, the north-eastern terminus of the Piccadilly line. A typical Holden design, it was opened in July 1933. The line was originally intended to extend further into the Essex countryside but green-belt legislation prevented this.

'BACK ROOM BOYS'

BUS MAINTENANCE

'THEY ALSO SERVE'

PUBLIC TRANSPORT AT WAR

WHATEVER OTHERS HOPED, or pretended, by 1937–8 the LPTB had little doubt that war was on its way, and that within days the capital might well be subjected to a terrible aerial bombardment. In the spring of 1939 a meeting at the Ministry of Transport finalised a long-prepared evacuation plan, and although war was not declared until 3 September, the evacuation began to be put into effect on the first of the month. In four days some 1,218,000, people – the majority school children and their teachers – had left the city. They were conveyed in 4,985 LPTB buses, 533 trams and 377 trolleybuses, mostly to seventy-two Underground stations and 129 'entraining main-line stations' out in the suburbs in order not to bring services at the main-line termini grinding to a halt. Sometimes the buses made much longer journeys, taking the children deep into the countryside, and there were instances of drivers being on duty, without sleep, for forty-eight hours.

Although the expected raids did not materialise for another year, transport restrictions of many sorts were imposed on the declaration of war. Green Line services ceased and 477 coaches were converted within two days into ambulances while, when the USA entered the war, another fifty-five became Clubmobiles, fitted out as mobile canteens and staffed by the Red Cross. They were named after American states and cities. Blackout was imposed on 1 September 1939, which made driving at night very hazardous, and the accident rate increased greatly. Four months after the Blitz

A Second World War poster featuring men and women working together, maintaining an STL double-deck bus.

Crowds watch a military parade at West Croydon during the 'phoney war' of late 1939 – the time from September until April the following year when little seemed to be happening. A Feltham and two E1 trams (the latter not yet fitted with windscreens) and a Country Area front-entrance STL, setting out on its long journey to Guildford, are forced to wait.

began, in September 1940, the *Hackney Gazette* reported that '19,545 civilians have been killed as the result of bombing … compared with a total of 11,434 deaths on the road … an increase of nearly 40 per cent on the corresponding (pre-war) period.' There were instances of trams bumping unseen into each other when an air raid was in progress and the electrical supply had been cut, and arrangements were quickly made to fit emergency lights back and front.

Many buses were taken off the road to conserve fuel, although they were soon to be reinstated, for, with private motoring virtually banned, the demand on public transport increased enormously. Posters exhorted people not to travel unless it was 'absolutely necessary' and certainly far fewer ventured out in the evenings, particularly once the Blitz began. The tram replacement programme ended in 1940 'for the duration'; indeed wherever possible trams and trolleybuses replaced motor bus services in order to conserve precious supplies of imported petrol and diesel.

Buses were lent to London from all over the United Kingdom, although this may have been more a gesture of solidarity with the suffering capital rather than a strict necessity. Later London would return the compliment, sending buses to many hard-pressed locations, such as Coventry and Glasgow, whose fleets suffered significant losses at the hands of Goering's Luftwaffe.

Initially, once the air-raid sirens sounded, drivers were ordered to stop their vehicles and, with their conductors, lead passengers to the nearest shelters, but after a while this changed. One driver stated, 'I never believed in parking up a bus as I considered it was in Mr Hitler's favour to do so. I always considered in driving a bus I had a weapon of war in my hand and it was up to me to use it to advantage against the enemy.' Many considered that it was safer to remain in a bus and particularly a solidly built tram than to head through the streets to find a shelter. However, one of the greatest dangers was from flying glass, even if the vehicle had not suffered a direct hit, and terrible injuries were caused. To counteract this, anti-blast netting was stuck to the windows and a small

Evacuees from a girl's school board three trams in south-east London on 2 September 1939, on their way to a mainline railhead and safety from the expected imminent aerial bombardment of the capital.

diamond shape was left clear in the centre so that passengers could see where they were.

For most people, when considering the LPTB's contribution to the war effort, it is the Underground and the safety provided by its stations which springs to mind. Initially the LPTB put up notices forbidding them to be used in this way but they were ignored. Even before the Blitz began on 7 September 1940 the *Ilford Recorder* noted: 'Amazing scenes have been witnessed at Tube tunnels and subways, which have become something in the nature of human dormitories. As soon as the black-out hour arrives there begins a trek of scores of people who have no shelters.' Two weeks later the *South London Press* recorded, 'Early every evening queues of families ... stand in line four or five deep. Police had to guard the doors since crowds have tried to rush the barriers as the sirens sounded.' Down on the platforms 'hundreds of men and women were partially undressed, while small boys and girls slumbered in the fetid atmosphere, absolutely naked. When a train came in it had to be stopped while police and porters went along pushing in the feet and arms which overhung the line.' On the train the reporter sat opposite a pilot on leave. 'He looked dumbly at that amazing platform. "It's the same all the way along," was all he said.'

In typical fashion the LPTB accepted the situation and set about organizing it. Special toilets were provided for the Tube, which was below the level of the sewers; food trains, staffed by the Women's Voluntary Services, ran to split-second schedules within the regular timetable; some of the regular occupiers of specific stations even produced newspapers; and joint Christian and Jewish religious services were held in the East End. However, not even Underground stations were totally safe and when a bomb penetrated the concourse of Bank Station on 29 December 1940, fifty-six people were killed. A similar number – the precise figure was never determined – died when a bomb at Balham pierced a water main and

flooded the Northern line Tube station. Worst of all was the incident at Bethnal Green Station, on the Central line, on 3 March 1943 when a huge explosion, ironically caused by the testing of a new British gun nearby, caused a panic. Crowds of people rushed down narrow, badly lit steps, stumbling and falling upon one another in the process, and within seconds 173 were crushed to death.

Although AEC and the LPTB's Chiswick Works were too occupied with war work to build more than a handful of replacements (the LPTB helped build over seven hundred Halifax bombers), non-standard and very basic buses, often with wooden seats and sometimes painted brown or grey all over when supplies of red ran out, were built by Guy, Daimler and Bristol to supplement the fleet, while trolleybuses destined for South Africa were diverted to East London.

Two LPTB depot staff contemplate the remains of trams wrecked by a direct German hit on Camberwell depot on 8 September 1940. In all twenty-nine cars were destroyed.

Women filled many of the jobs done before the war by men, ranging from conductors to mechanics and even working on the LPTB farms in Essex. None were ever employed as bus drivers in London, although they were elsewhere. Astonishing feats of bravery were performed by staff; merely taking a vehicle out in the Blitz night after night required steady nerves and much more. The traditional British upper lip was no cliché. Typical was a guard at Baker Street station who described how his supper was interrupted by incendiary bombs falling on the station. At considerable danger to himself he managed to put them out but complained that afterwards, 'I found my supper was spoilt and the tea cold.'

Many employees of all ranks served in the forces or in various government roles. The expertise acquired over long years by senior officials would prove invaluable in their later positions in government. J. P. Thomas, who had just retired as general manager of London Transport Railways, was appointed supremo to liaise between the government, local

Regent Street, seen from Piccadilly Circus in late 1945. The buses and taxis are all of pre-war vintage except for the one immediately ahead of the number 60, which is a wartime austerity Daimler double-decker.

The LPTB helped to build hundreds of Halifax heavy bombers during the war. After a shift, workers climb into an STL, which has many of its shattered windows boarded up.

authorities and the LPTB. Frank Pick left the LPTB in 1940 and became director general of the Ministry of Information but fell out with Churchill over whether it was legitimate for propaganda to be economical with the truth: when Pick stated that he had never knowingly told a lie and was not going to start then, Churchill exploded and declared that he never wanted to see 'that impeccable busman' again. Pick died of a cerebral hemorrhage on 7 November 1941. It is no exaggeration to claim that the LPTB was his, more than anyone else's, creation.

One of Chiswick's most senior engineers, Jack Lemmer, had joined up at the outbreak of war but was called into the office of a high government official and told that he was needed back at Chiswick Works to head the team working on alternative ways of powering buses other than by precious imported petrol or diesel. The result was a gas-producing trailer which was towed behind a bus. It was far from an unqualified success, being temperamental and unable to generate much more than half the normal power, and was therefore restricted to operating on routes devoid of severe gradients. But every gallon of fuel saved was vital.

Jack Lemmer at the age of ninety-nine in 2006. He began work as an apprentice engineer with London General in 1923, moved on to the central works at Chiswick where he met a number of 'marvellous engineers', and set up his own business in 1946.

Opposite bottom: Guy Arab No. G351 – the only surviving complete London bus built to wartime austerity standards, which actually entered service in 1946.

An ST powered by a gas-producing trailer of the type developed by Jack Lemmer.

At all levels LPTB staff made Herculean efforts to keep services running. Buses often appeared with boards replacing glass in shattered windows, overhauls were delayed, minimum destination details became the order of the day, paintwork grew shabbier and shabbier, but somehow services were maintained come what may. Croydon Garage received two direct hits on the night of 10 May 1941 resulting in the deaths of seven men and the destruction of sixty-five buses. Yet by mid-morning on the 11 May a sufficient number of buses had been requisitioned from other garages to run almost a full service on all the Croydon routes.

By the end of the war 422 LPTB staff had been killed and 2,873 injured. A total of 166 buses and coaches, sixty trams, fifteen trolleybuses and nineteen Underground carriages had been destroyed and many thousands damaged but patched up and returned to service.

Many vehicles were still operating that should have been retired but valiant efforts had kept them in service. Unlike at the end of the First World War, there was no shortage of work for returning servicemen, whose skills were needed to restore London Transport to the pre-eminent position it had enjoyed in September 1939.

Above: LPTB conductresses on the roof of the LPTB headquarters, just before the Victory Parade.

AT YOUR SERVICE

He does a difficult job with patience and understanding. He is one of 22,000 conductors who issue nearly ten million tickets to travellers on London Transport road vehicles every day.

RECOVERY

THE LPTB WAS faced with a huge backlog of maintenance and replacement of worn-out and time-expired vehicles and rolling stock as the war in Europe came to an end in August 1945. Between November 1945 and October 1949 1,106 buses, some over fifteen years old, were sent to outside contractors to have their bodies renovated so they could keep going until replacements became available.

On the Underground the New Works Programme, halted by the outbreak of war, was resumed, the cost having risen to £50 million. In December 1946 the first eastward extension of the Central line was opened, followed by others until Epping was reached in September 1949. Westwards West Ruislip was reached in November 1948. However, further planned extensions out into the countryside never materialised with green-belt legislation and the creation of new towns such as Crawley and Basildon, and this meant that Aldenham depot, north-east of Watford, would never serve as a Northern line depot but would instead be the bus body overhaul works and would become a pilgrimage site for Cliff Richard fans after featuring in his film *Summer Holiday*. Chiswick Works from now on would concentrate on overhauling chassis, while all bus bodies would be built by contractors, chiefly Park Royal and Weymann.

The war meant that only 151 of the next standard double-deck bus, the RT, had been built. In 1944 the LPTB had put in an order for one thousand RTs and had been promised

A 1947 Leo Dowd poster demonstrating the work of the bus conductor; note the early post-war Veronica Lake-inspired hairstyle of one of the passengers.

Poster dating from 1949 advertising extensions to the Central line.

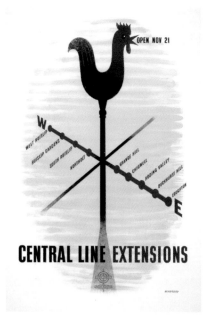

that the first would arrive at the end of 1945, but this proved much too optimistic and the LPTB had to make do with a small number of AEC and Leyland double- and single-deck buses of more or less standard provincial design. It was a great day when eventually RT402, with a Weymann body, began operating on 10 May 1947, followed thirteen days later by RT152 with an effectively identical Park Royal body. Production was slow at first but as post-war restrictions on material were eased and the urgent cry 'Export or Die!' became less strident it increased.

On 1 January 1948 the London Passenger Transport Board ceased to exist and was replaced by the London Transport Executive, part of the nationalised British Transport

Central Area red RT from Catford Garage and two green Country Area RTs from Godstone Garage at West Croydon in 1959.

Commission, although the general public would not have noticed any difference. Lord Ashfield had retired in 1947 and died the following year; he was succeeded as chairman by Lord Latham, formerly leader of London County Council.

The Leyland version of the RT, the RTL, appeared in 1948, and 755 new double-deckers

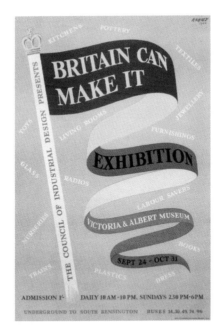

A poster for the 'Britain Can Make It' exhibition at the Victoria and Albert Museum in 1946, looking forward to a bright new innovative future, organised by the Council of Industrial Design and inspired by Frank Pick's pioneering efforts.

took to the road in that year, their bodies also supplied by Cravens and Saunders. But this provision did not even keep pace with the withdrawal of worn-out pre-war vehicles, and brand-new ECW-bodied Bristols intended for the provinces were diverted to London as a stop-gap measure while a huge variety of often ancient but roadworthy coaches and single- and double-deck buses was hired in from various sources. There was no more talk, for the moment, of getting rid of the remaining trams, which, although elderly, on passing through Charlton Works could be made serviceable for a few more years. Seventy-seven new Q1 trolleybuses, updated versions of the pre-war standard, arrived in 1948, followed by a final fifty in 1952; there would be no more.

Petrol, like so much else, was still rationed but there was full employment, people had money and demands on public transport were greater than ever. London Transport was able to revert to the pre-war practice of introducing a summer timetable when services were increased to cope with

London Transport actively recruited employees from the Caribbean in the 1950s in order to keep bus, trolleybus and Underground services running.

the crowds heading for the countryside, and red Central Area buses were drafted in on Sundays to help out – for many people still worked on Saturday until lunchtime. London Transport actively recruited employees from the Caribbean who joined in large numbers in the 1950s and 1960s. Invaluable though they were, they met with considerable racial prejudice, sometimes within London Transport but more commonly outside. Yet their contribution to creating the modern London – described as 'a vibrant city that now speaks more than 300 languages' by Sir Peter Hendy CBE (commissioner, TfL) in 2013 – was vital.

Two more versions of the RT appeared in 1949: the SRT, an ill-judged and short-lived conversion of the STL chassis with a standard RT body, which proved to be underpowered with inadequate brakes; and the excellent RTW, an 8-foot wide version of the RTL, with body as well as chassis built by Leyland,

Kingston Bus Station and Garage in 1976 with two of the long-lived RFs: London Transport's standard single-deck bus of the 1950s.

the body being a remarkably good imitation of the standard version. In 1949 1,592 new double-deckers entered service in London, which wasn't far short of the total fleet of Midland Red, the next biggest bus company in the UK. Production of the RT family continued until 1954, by which time close on seven thousand had been built, although not all had been in service at the same time. The single-deck version, the RF, which was an AEC mark IV Regal with its engine under the floor and the direct successor of the pre-war Q, entered service in 1951 and by 1954 had an almost complete monopoly of Green Line and Central and Country Area bus services.

By the mid 1950s London Transport was entering uncertain times. Private motoring was growing apace and people's habits were changing, such as watching television in the evening. London Transport realised it had overestimated its needs and a number of new RTs and RTLs went straight into store and were only gradually put into service. They replaced earlier examples of the same types and these were eagerly snapped up secondhand.

RTL1610 heads across Lambeth Bridge on 21 March 1959. This Leyland version of the RT was one of the last built, in 1954, but did not enter service until 1958 and is still bereft of advertisements.

The traffic grows, and the Londoner's dependence on his public transport grows, too ⊖ New circumstances need new techniques, new methods ⊖ New automatically-driven trains for the Victoria Line ⊖ New buses for London's Red Arrow and flat-fare routes ⊖ New machines for automatic fare collection to save staff on road and rail ⊖ More station car parks ⊖ London Transport must change to keep pace with the constantly changing pattern of London on the move ⊖

UNCERTAIN TIMES

B Y 1950 A sufficient number of new buses was entering the
fleet for the final withdrawal of the trams to begin, and
on 30 September that year the Wandsworth and Battersea
area routes went over to motor buses. It had already been
announced that there would be no more trolleybuses and,
one trolleybus route, the 612, was also replaced. The tram-
abandonment programme continued, and larger and larger
crowds appeared as each suburb said goodbye, part in
celebration, part in regret. Trams were generally seen as old-
fashioned and the cause of traffic congestion, and although
some brave souls argued against this, citing growing pollution
by the petrol and diesel engine and the desire of practically
every household to possess its own private car, they were
ignored. By 6 July 1952 the tram had vanished from the
streets of London. The magnificent Felthams found a new
home in Leeds, as did No.1, intended by the London County
Council in 1932 to be the precursor of a fleet of revolutionary
new cars – a fleet which never materialised.

However, there was still plenty of electric transport with an
expanding future in London in the shape of the Underground.
New R stock trains, which looked identical to the newest pre-
war cars, began to arrive in 1949 for the District line, fitted
with fluorescent lighting, enabling the ancient, wooden-
bodied pre-1914 vehicles with hand-operated doors, which
had a disconcerting habit of gradually opening as the trains
rattled through the dark, to be withdrawn. Tube trains

A poster from
around 1970
featuring two
new types of
vehicles: the
successful Tube
train and what
would turn
out to be the
disastrously
misjudged
high-capacity
Merlin one-man-
operated single-
deck bus.

replaced steam on the remote, rural single-track Epping to Ongar branch in 1957, and new stock began to work on the Central and Piccadilly lines at the end of 1959. Widening of the Metropolitan line out to Northwood Hills was completed in September 1961, and the steam era on the Underground, apart from engineers' trains, ended on 12 September 1960 when the Chesham branch was electrified. New trains continued to appear on the Underground: the A60 stock of 248 cars on the Metropolitan line in 1961, then the A62 on the District; these were less striking than their flared predecessors but destined to be long-lived. More Central line trains in 1962 enabled the last pre-LPTB (standard Tube stock) to be withdrawn in early 1963. The Metropolitan electric locomotives ceased work in September 1961, EMUs (electrical multiple unit trains) being the universal norm from then on. Red had long been the traditional livery for all Underground trains but the aluminium-bodied R stock trains were unpainted except for a red stripe, and this set the pattern for future vehicles, both surface and Tube. However, decades later this would be modified and in the twenty-first century all new Tube and surface trains have sported significant areas of traditional red.

In September 1962 work began on a brand new Tube line, the £56-million Victoria

A poster marking the final opening of the Victoria line in 1971, the first entirely new Tube line since Edwardian times.

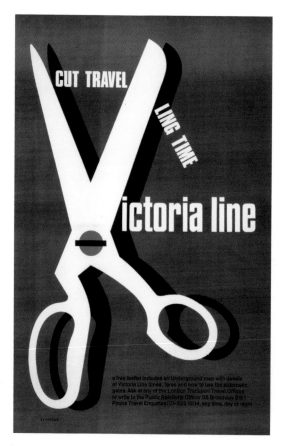

CUT TRAVEL

LING TIME

ictoria line

a free leaflet includes an Underground map with details of Victoria Line times, fares and how to use the automatic gates. Ask at any of the London Transport Travel Offices or write to the Public Relations Officer 55 Broadway SW1 Phone Travel Enquiries: 01-222 1234, any time, day or night line from Walthamstow to Brixton – the Underground had always been conspicuous by its absence south of the River. It opened in sections and was completed in July 1971. Experiments in automation of ticket issuing began in 1964. The old Metropolitan Railway generating station at Neasden closed in July 1968, and from then on power came from Lots Road, Chelsea, and the old LCC tramway power station at Greenwich; eventually the National Grid would take over. Control of the Tube was becoming more automated, a new £70-million centre opening at Euston.

By the late 1960s Heathrow had become the busiest airport in the world, and in April 1971 work began on an extension of the Piccadilly line to serve it. It would open to Heathrow Central in December 1977. The 1970s saw more and more new rolling stock, both for the Tube and the surface lines, and construction of another new Tube line, the Fleet (renamed the Jubilee Line in 1977 to commemorate the Queen's Silver Jubilee), began in February 1972.

There are few safer methods of transport than the London Underground, despite not always being the most comfortable or pleasurable experience in the rush hour. There have been three serious losses of life since the 1960s. On 28 February 1975 a Northern City line train inexplicably failed to slow down as it entered the terminus at Moorgate and slammed

PICCADILLY LINE TO HEATHROW AIRPORT

1977 -1997

A poster commemorating twenty years of the Piccadilly line extension to Heathrow Airport.

Routemasters at Oxford Circus in 1979. The type served central London for some fifty years, the last surviving in Oxford Street until December 2005.

into the end wall, killing the driver and forty-two passengers. On 18 November 1987 debris beneath an escalator at Kings Cross caught fire, causing thirty-one deaths. Shortly after this smoking was banned everywhere on the Underground. On 7 July 2005 British-born terrorists set off four bombs: three on the Underground, one on a No. 30 bus. Apart from the four bombers, fifty-two passengers died. Their names and the reason they were in London at the time – whether visitors, students, professionals or workers on London's transport system – reflected how London had become a city that welcomed people from all over the world. An Alexander Dennis Enviro 400 double-deck bus was named Spirit of London as a memorial to those who were murdered.

A brand-new Routemaster, RML894, on trolleybus replacement service at Finchley, 8 November 1961. There is still work, for a few more months, for L3 trolleybus No.1449 behind.

The last moments of a Dartford area trolleybus at the scrapyard at Charlton in April 1959, at the beginning of the programme which saw the world's largest trolleybus network disappear from the streets of London. With virtually no secondhand market for trolleybuses, almost all were disposed of in this fashion.

Before the last RTs entered service, the prototypes of their successor, the Routemaster, had arrived. By the 1950s travel on public transport was in decline and saving fuel was imperative. In the provinces lightweight, sparsely fitted-out buses were often the order of the day, not exactly conducive to passenger comfort, but in London the Routemaster, although no heavier than an RT, could carry eight more passengers with no sacrifice in comfort. Of AEC manufacture, naturally, with a Park Royal body, the production vehicles began to replace the trolleybus fleet in November 1959.

Like the trams a decade earlier no sentiment or time was wasted in disposing of them, the very last, based at Isleworth and Fulwell, going on the night of 8/9 May 1962. The post-war Q1s, good for many years' service yet, were sold to Spain and a few examples, like the trams, have been preserved.

There were those who considered that London Transport had lost the creative, dynamic spark it had demonstrated throughout the 1930s, the Routemaster being an example of this. Innovative in a number of ways, with an aluminium body and with improved suspension and transmission, it didn't look revolutionary with its half-cab layout and open-rear platform. And Leyland was about to reveal the rear-engined Atlantean which would utterly transform the

British double-deck bus scene. Only time would tell what a remarkable investment the Routemaster was. Production continued, although at nothing like the rate of the RT at its height. Replacement now began of the RT family, the great majority being sold for service elsewhere in the UK and abroad. But it would be decades before the last RT left regular passenger service in London.

Similarly there was nothing to match the superb buildings of the Holden era, the one exception being Stockwell Bus Garage, with its great sweeping, reinforced concrete arches, but even this happened by accident, steel being in short supply. Designed by Adie, Button and Partners, it is now a listed Grade II* building. Otherwise, the stations for the Victoria line, for instance, although workmanlike, lacked the flair and élan of earlier examples.

An announcer at Tower Hill Underground Station. By the 1960s more and more women were being employed in a greater variety of roles on London Transport.

Two RTs on a busy road in Barking, 1978.

A batch of Routemasters, the RMLs, now stretched to 30 feet to enable them to seat seventy-two passengers, replacing the Finchley trolleybuses in November 1961; and, from July 1965 until production ended at the beginning of 1968, the RML became the standard. Coach versions of both the short and long Routemaster were built and were probably the most comfortable vehicles ever offered to Green Line passengers. Sadly numbers of the latter diminished, with the Green Line network in serious decline, and the Routemaster coaches were eventually downgraded to buses.

A driver and a conductor coming off duty at Barking in 1978. In the background are three generations of double-deckers: an RT, a Routemaster and a DMS.

Congestion was growing, not just in central London but in the suburbs, too, with more and more passengers deserting the bus in favour of their own personal transport. Various solutions were suggested, and routes were shortened and broken into sections in order to reduce delays. Working for London Transport was no longer a high-status job; better-paid employment, without unsociable hours, was not hard to find. The unions called strikes but these only aggravated the problems as passengers found alternative means of getting to and from work and never went back to the buses. London Transport seemed to be losing its way.

£280

Travel to work for less.

OXFORD STREET

NITY
T

RE
ST

⊖ TRAVELCARD ⊖   25

And to the shops for nothing

If you take the Bus or Tube to work, you're most bound to be better off with a Travelcard. Not only is it normally cheaper than buying daily tickets it's also far more flexible. You can use your Travelcard at any time n any Tube or Bus* in the Zones it covers.

So apart from saving money getting to work, you can also go shopping at lunchtime without spending a penny.

LONDON TRANSPORT
Travelcard
ALL ZONES

Expires

See over

RAVELCARD. JUST THE TICKET FOR GETTING AROUND LONDON.

WHICH DIRECTION?

O VER THE YEARS the amalgamation of the Central and Country Areas had been mooted but never pursued. Instead, 1 January 1970 saw the complete separation of the two: the biggest change to London Transport since its founding in 1933. The process had begun in 1965 at the time of the formation of the Greater London Council. Four years later it took over control of London Transport from the British Transport Commission, with the understanding that the Country Area was none of its business and that this should pass to the National Bus Company, assuming the title London Country. In practice London Country found itself faced with all sorts of problems. Much of the administration and engineering areas of the Country Area had been integrated with the Central Area; all these had to be unscrambled and, although throughout much of 1969 a group had been looking at these issues, many had not yet been resolved. Chiswick and Aldenham continued for a time to overhaul London Country vehicles and London Transport provided support for London Country in various other ways, the most long-lasting being the servicing of ticket machines for a further ten years.

Not least of the new company's problems was that the decline in patronage was greater in its area than in that retained by London Transport, and it would run into all sorts of trouble through the 1970s and '80s. A total of 1,267 buses and coaches departed with the setting up of London Country. These were nearly all RTs, Routemasters and RFs

The one-day Travelcard was introduced in 1984; a Monopoly board, with a Routemaster on Oxford Street and a Tube train on Piccadilly, was used to promote it.

Border country: there were many places where London buses encountered those of other companies. Here a Leyland National from London Country meets Southend Corporation and Eastern National double-deckers at Grays in Essex, six years after London Country was founded.

– excellent vehicles but designed for a different era, and they needed to be replaced as soon as possible; some RTs and many Routemasters found their way back into the London Transport fold. Eventually the National Bus Company was sold off and London Country split into myriad organisations so that today it is almost impossible to recognise its origins.

London Transport employed its first woman bus driver, Jill Viner, in June 1974 . The number of passengers using London buses was still in decline and the high-capacity, one-person-operated single-decker was seen as the solution. London Transport invested heavily in the AEC Merlin and the shorter version, the Swift from 1966. It was probably the worst decision it ever made. The first were used on the new Red Arrow 500 express rush-hour service between Victoria and Marble Arch

One of the disastrous AEC Swifts, SMS821 of 1971, alongside an ever-reliable RT4795, in George Street, Croydon, 1973.

DMS2295 in Katharine Street, Croydon, in 1978, soon after entering service. These handsome one-person-operated buses with London Transport-designed bodies on Daimler chassis proved a very poor investment, some lasting little more than five years.

and performed reasonably well but the production ones which started work on twenty-two routes in September 1968 proved unreliable and unsuitable for London conditions.

By the beginning of the 1970s they were failing in huge numbers and the faithful RT had to be kept running far longer than intended. It was the end of the road for AEC, a sad dying fall to a glittering career as the provider of the London bus ever since Edwardian days. AEC was part of the Leyland empire and that, too, was in terminal decline.

In 1970 the first production one-person double-decker, the DMS, a Daimler rear-engined bus with an LT-designed body, entered service. By the end of the year 1,967 were on order. Yet it proved little better than the Swift or Merlin. London Transport was, indeed, in deep trouble. By the time the RT finally bowed out in 1979 the first DMSs had been withdrawn.

The era of the unique London bus, designed specifically for service in the capital seemed to be over with somewhat modified but nevertheless basically provincial-style Leyland Titans and MCW Metrobuses proving a much better investment than the Merlin, Swift or DMS. The Routemaster began to be phased out in 1982, but most examples were still in excellent condition

London Transport's first woman bus driver, Jill Viner, taking up work at Norbiton Garage in June 1974.

Left: The single-deck AEC Swifts of 1970 proved even more unreliable than the DMSs and some did not survive their first overhaul. At the back of Norbiton Garage in 1980, this one is waiting to be scrapped.

Right:
A twenty-six-seat Bristol/ECW BL17 heading through leafy Dulwich towards Brixton in 1977.

and were bought and put into service all over the UK and abroad. This was the beginning of an afterlife which still continues, the bus being regarded as a symbol of London and used as a sightseeing vehicle in locations across the globe as varied as California, Niagara Falls, Helsinki, New Zealand and Moscow. In the event London Transport realised that one-person operation was unsuitable for the most heavily used central London routes, the Routemaster was reprieved, and with various re-enginings and refurbishments was able to virtually monopolise central London routes into the twenty-first century.

In 1988 the London Regional Business Plan established eleven management bus units within London Transport, but this was merely the prelude to privatisation. These units then bid for the routes they wished to operate – competitive tendering as it was termed. Beyond London, deregulation – described as 'the development of competition' by the Conservative minister,

A Transdev Dennis Dart, a tremendously successful single-deck design, at Heathrow.

Nicholas Ridley, who was enthusiastically driving it forward – was proceeding apace and was expected eventually to reach the capital. It never did, to the relief of all those who believed that it would have caused chaos.

In 1983 London Transport celebrated its Golden Jubilee in great style with buses, mostly Routemasters, decked out in gold, in replica 1933 liveries and other eye-catching colours. A two-day festival was held at Chiswick Works in July. It would be Chiswick's swansong for, with privatisation, the works would become redundant; it is now a business park although the adjacent Acton Underground Works still operates.

One-person operation had both saved money and slowed down services but methods were now being developed of paying for travel without having to pay the driver or conductor every time you boarded a bus. By the 1980s the decline in bus and Underground travel had been halted, not least because, as congestion grew worse, restrictions were being placed on where the private car could operate and park; these restrictions were largely supported by the public, who were increasingly worried about the damage emissions were causing to the environment.

Opposite: The famous Chiswick Works skidpan in operation in 1983, with an RT displaying its skating abilities.

ALL
round

YOUR NEIGHBOURHOOD. All round town. And now.
all ROUND THE CLOCK.

LET'S ALL KEEP THE ARTERIES CLEAR

BUSES ARE THE LIFEBLOOD OF LONDON

Our five thousand buses run on five hundred routes on 1,880 miles of road to take you
to every part of London. And now, thanks to Night Buses it's a round the clock service.
Just like our travel information service. Ring 071-222 1234 any time of day or night

THE GOOD TIMES RETURN

Tᴴᴇ ᴏɴᴄᴇ-ᴅᴇꜱᴘɪꜱᴇᴅ ᴛʀᴀᴍ had begun to make a return, worldwide, in the 1970s and the Docklands Light Railway (DLR) which opened in 1987, had certain tramway-like characteristics, notably the vehicles and some very sharp bends and severe gradients. Remotely controlled without drivers, it was built to serve the area east of the Tower, once the heart of London Docks but now transformed into a business centre with some spectacular, high-rise offices.

Today it has six branches, covering 25 miles, and carries an average of three-hundred thousand passengers each day; for 2011 the total number of passengers was eighty-six million. Street-running trams returned in 2000. Tramlink, based in Croydon, runs partly over former railway lines, partly in streets and partly on reserved roadside track

Opposite:
A late-1960s poster promoting all-night bus travel and featuring a Routemaster and a DMS.

Original and 2007-vintage Docklands Light Railway trains pass near East India Dock, September 2010.

Right: A publicity leaflet for the Millennium Dome in the year 2000.

Opposite: A new train of S stock, dating from 2013, leaving Hammersmith for the City. Its connections are so wide the eight cars look like one continuous unit.

to New Addington, Elmers End, Beckenham Junction and Wimbledon.

London Buses Ltd was privatised between January 1994 and January 1995. For a time all sorts of liveries appeared but it was soon realised that the red so long associated with the London bus was iconic and the edict went out that the London bus had to be red. In 1995 the first 'kneeling' bus, able to lower itself at bus stops, appeared, making it much easier for elderly passengers and mothers with buggies to enter at virtually kerb level, and all buses are now of this configuration.

How to get to the Dome by public transport

The Millennium Experience at the Dome, Greenwich

Metropolitan Railway 0-4-4T No.1 about to set off from a snowy Olympia Station on a trip around the Circle line to commemorate the 150th anniversary of the world's first underground railway, January 2013.

The world's first 'hybrid' double-decker, basically an electric bus powered by a diesel electric engine, entered service in London in January 2007, and many more have followed – a big step in reducing pollution.

London Transport, no longer a commercial organisation, was replaced in 2000 by Transport for London (TfL) with a remit to implement transport strategy and manage services across London.

Divided into three main directorates, these are: (1) London Underground; (2) Surface Transport: for buses, black cabs, river services, dial-a-ride, congestion charge and London's strategic road network; and (3) London Rail, which includes the Docklands Light Railway, London Overground and Croydon Tramlink.

Below: Two of the Bombardier-built Tramlink cars in George Street, Croydon, 2010.

Its latest charge is Crossrail, the long-awaited underground link right through the heart of London from west to east, designed to take normal-size trains. Begun in 2009, it is Europe's largest construction project, with the first section scheduled to open in 2017. The overground provision dates from 2007 which has given TfL some control

The Tottenham Court Road works for Crossrail, the largest intersection on the network, with an LT-type new Routemaster passing, January 2014.

not only of the Underground but also surface rail transport in the capital. It consists of six lines and eighty-three stations and patronage on all its routes has skyrocketed. Nevertheless, buses still carry more passengers than rail routes.

The Commissioner for Transport is Sir Peter Hendy CBE, who was knighted for the way TfL coped with organising transport in London during the 2012 Olympics. Head of Surface Transport is Leon Daniels. The success of TfL in the twenty-first century is due to many factors, not least to the

In its continuing quest to reduce pollution, TfL has recently introduced eight hydrogen buses that emit nothing but water. They operate route RV1 between Covent Garden (seen here) and Tower Gateway.

vision of these two men, reminding many of the great days of Ashfield and Pick. Perhaps not surprisingly both are also dyed-in-the-wool transport enthusiasts: Leon Daniels was one of the earliest members of the London Bus Preservation Trust, based at Brooklands, Surrey, and the custodian of a unique collection of historic London public transport vehicles. Sixty-three years after Pick's death, Thomas Heatherwick, designer of the 'New Bus for London', wrote: 'Transport for London is now reaffirming its commitment to the original values of transport

Sir Peter Hendy CBE, Commissioner for Transport in London until 2015, and Leon Daniels, Head of Surface Transport, in front of one of the new LT-type New Routemasters, 2012.

commissioning established by Pick more than half a century ago ... We are proud to have contributed something to the continuation of Frank Pick's enduring legacy.'

Another place where the history of public transport is on display in considerable depth is the official TfL collection in Covent Garden. Elsewhere are museums where one can ride on preserved London trams and trolleybuses, and literally thousands of London buses are preserved worldwide.

To a lot of people's surprise, London once again has its own, purpose-built double-deck bus – the New Routemaster – mooted by Mayor Boris Johnson, designed by Thomas Heatherwick and built by Wrightbus of Ballymena,

A model of a possible Underground train of the future.

Northern Ireland. On starting service in 2012, it attracted huge attention, the travelling public sensing that here was something startlingly new, yet with deliberate echoes of London bus history. Equally startling and much admired are the stations built for the £3.2-billion Jubilee line extension, completed in December 1999 and evoking another great station designer, James Holden.

Tickets are becoming a thing of the past as far as bus and train travel is concerned. There is the one-day Travelcard while for regular travellers the Oyster card, rather like a credit card, was introduced in July 2003. By June 2012 forty-three million had been issued and it was used for more than eighty per cent of all journeys in London. It is possible nowadays to check by way of mobile phones and other technology when your next bus or train is due before ever leaving your house. Investment in public transport all over the UK is of supreme importance with a growing population and the urgent need to reduce emissions. With over half of all bus journeys in England currently made in London alone, it will remain critical for TfL to continue to find efficient, environmentally friendly ways of keeping Londoners on the move.

FURTHER READING

Akehurst, Laurie. *Country Buses: Volume 1 1933–1949.* Capital Transport, 2012.

Akehurst, Laurie. *Country Buses: Volume 2 1950–1959.* Capital Transport, 2014.

Baker, Michael H. C. *Lost Voices of the London Trams.* Ian Allan, 2014.

Baker, Michael H. C. *London Transport from the 1930s to the 1950s.* Ian Allan, 2009.

Blacker, Ken. *The London Trolleybus: Volume 1 1931–1945.* Capital Transport, 2002.

Blacker, Ken. *The London Trolleybus: Volume 2 1946–1962.* Capital Transport, 2004.

Green, Oliver. *Frank Pick's London.* V&A Publishing, 2013.

Millar, Alan (editor). *The London Bus: 80 Years of Capital Service.* Key Books, 2013.

Oakley, E. R. and Holland, C. E. *London Transport Tramways 1933–1952.* London Tramways History Group, 1999.

Taylor, Hugh. *London's Last Trams.* Adam Gordon, 2013.

Whiting, James, Booth, Gavin and Brown, Stewart J. *Boris's Bus.* Capital Transport, 2013.

The original London Transport logo has been adapted to serve many functions, as here for cycle hire, January 2014.

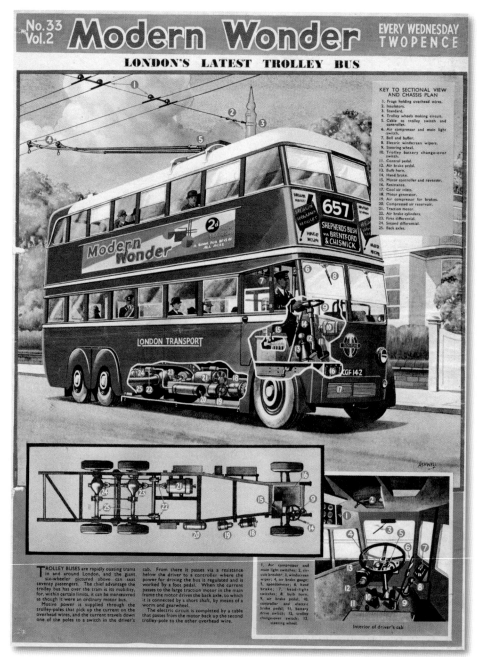

A delightful period illustration of one of the latest London C-class trolleybuses of 1936.

PLACES TO VISIT

London Transport Museum, Covent Garden, London WC2E
7BB. Telephone: 020 7379 6344.
Website: bookings@ltmuseum.co.uk
In the heart of London, the LTM contains a large part of
the official collection of vehicles and other items dating
from the 1930s and even before. There is also the reserve
collection held at Acton in west London, which is well
worth a visit but is open only on a few occasions each year.

The London Bus Museum, Brooklands Museum, Weybridge,
Surrey KT13 OQN. Telephone: 01932 837 994.
Website: www.Londonbusmuseum.com
Complementing the London Transport Museum, this is
the largest collection of London buses and coaches to be
found anywhere, dating back to the days of horse-drawn
buses. On special occasions it is possible to ride on a
vintage bus, and even sometimes on a horse-drawn one.
Throughout the year there are a number of special events
featuring visiting buses and coaches.

Sandtoft Trolley Bus Museum, Sandtoft near Doncaster,
Yorkshire DN8 5SX. Telephone: 01724 711391.
Website: trolleybusmuseum@sandtoft.org
The largest collection of trolleybuses in the world,
including several from London.

East Anglia Transport Museum, Carleton Colville, near
Lowestoft, Suffolk NR33 8BL. Telephone: 01502
518459. Website: eastangliatransportmuseum@live.co.uk
The only museum where it is possible to ride on both a
London tram and a trolleybus.

The National Tram Museum, Crich, Derbyshire DE4 5DP.
Telephone: 01773 854321. Email:enquiry@tramway.co.uk
A wonderfully comprehensive collection of trams from all
over the UK and from abroad, and the most comprehensive
collection of preserved and restored London trams.

INDEX